PARAGRAPH EDITING AND GRAMMAR CORRECTION WORKBOOK

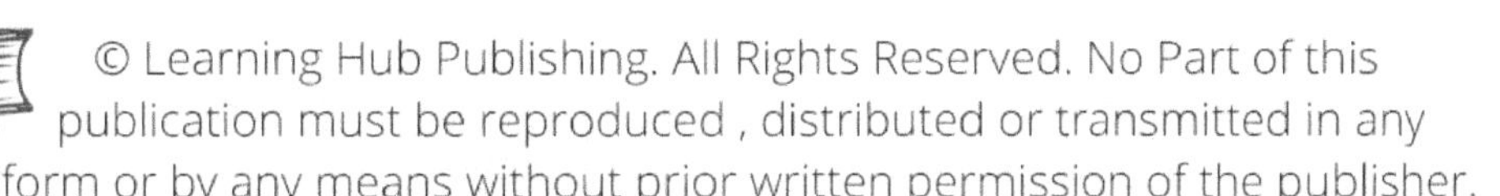

This Book Belongs to :

____

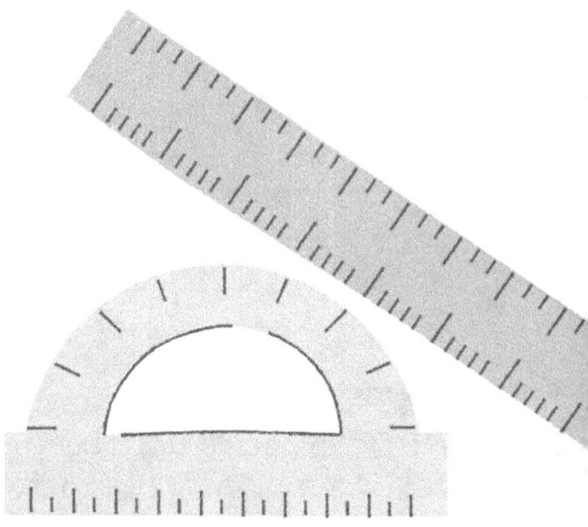

Find the Errors & Fix the Grammar

 Correct Spelling  Capitalize Letter  Add a question mark  Lowercase Letter  Add/Remove Letter or Word  Add a Period

Tom wanted to go outt and play basketball
So he went with his friends played for two
hourrs and then came back home by 7 PM.
After he coming back home his mom served
him dinner which he eaten quickly and then
tom slept.

 Correct Spelling   Capitalize Letter   Add a question mark   Lowercase Letter   Add/Remove Letter or Word   Add a Period

Tom wanted to go ~~outt~~ and play basketball.

So he went with his friend played for two

~~hourrs~~ and then came back home by 7 PM.

after he ~~coming~~ back home his mom served

him dinner which he ~~eaten~~ quickly and then

~~tom~~* slept.

Answer shown above as a Sample to show how to solve further Paragraphs which lie ahead.

1

Find the Errors & Fix the Grammar

I went sightseeing wthh my family and it was really fun, We got to sea different monuments and also big parks whrere we clicked a lot photographs and had some really nice fuod when we hungry.

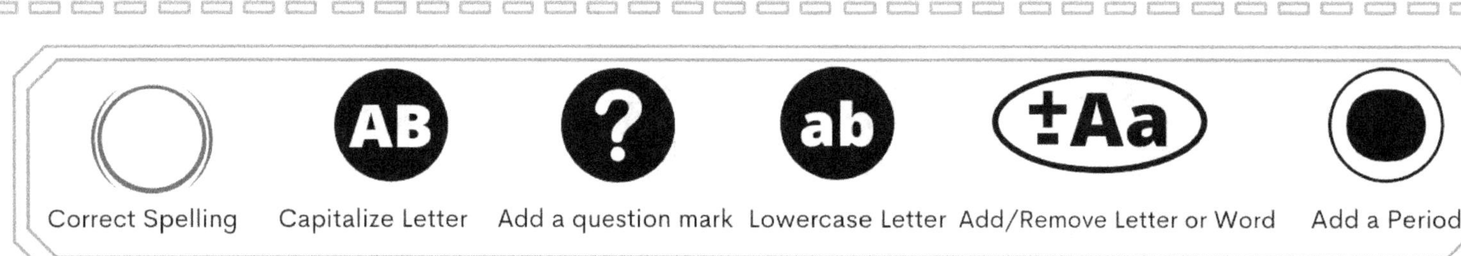

the lion is also known as the king of thE jungle. They are big and ferocious and hunt their pray with full force A person once asked me " How much do the lions weigh " to which I relpied "They can weigh as much as 190 kg when they reach adulthood".

Answers for all the paragraphs can be found from page 43.

2

 Correct Spelling    Capitalize Letter    Add a question mark    Lowercase Letter    Add/Remove Letter or Word    Add a Period

Today my mom made us pizza. She put a lot of chese which made it even more tasty. The funniest part is that while was eating the pizza it spilled all over my shirt and and we had to use detergent to clean it later.

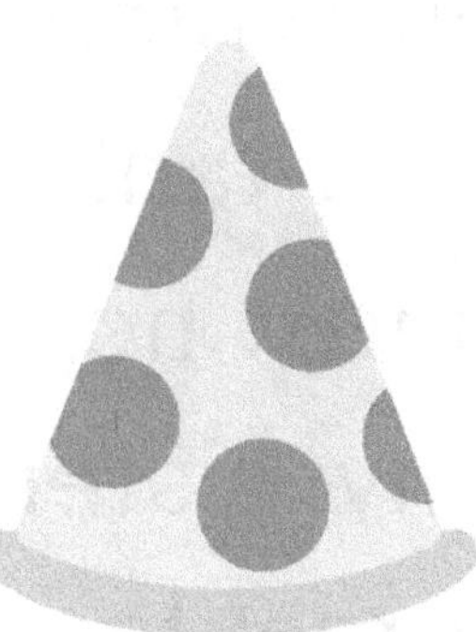

 Correct Spelling    Capitalize Letter    Add a question mark    Lowercase Letter    Add/Remove Letter or Word    Add a Period

While I was taking out my wallet what I noteds was that I had forgot to bring the exact change which needed to buy Milk. The cashier respectfully asked if I wanted to pay by card ?, But how could I tell him to him that the card is also at home

Find the Errors & Fix the Grammar

 Correct Spelling  Capitalize Letter  Add a question mark  Lowercase Letter  Add/Remove Letter or Word  Add a Period

me and my Sista recently bought a Fish tank in which we put a goldfish the day we got the tank. Our mom keeps telling us that we must not feed the glodfish so much food but my sister feels that the fish needs to eats breakfast lunch and dinner

---

 Correct Spelling  Capitalize Letter  Add a question mark  Lowercase Letter  Add/Remove Letter or Word 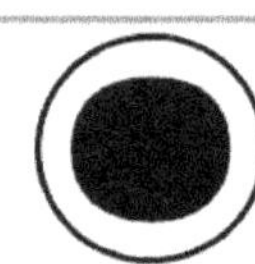 Add a Period

A bird landed on mine window and started pecking at my window without stopping, I quickly called my mother where which the noise was coming From. She quicklyy opened the window and gavethe bird some rice which it ate and then flew away.

Find the Errors & Fix the Grammar

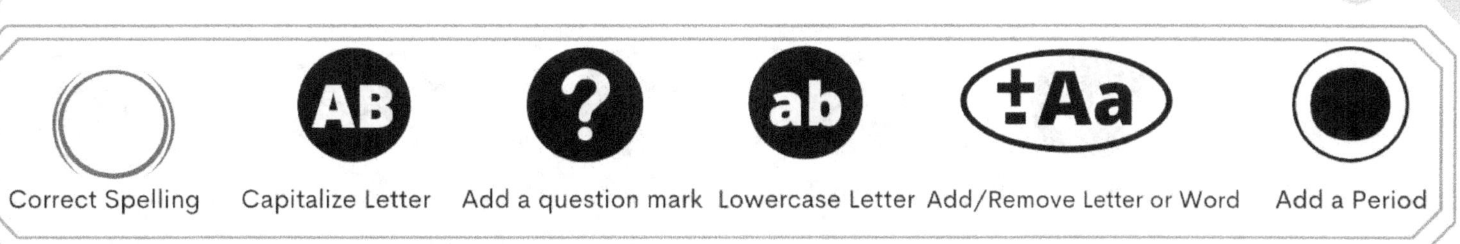

One day it was Raining very heavily and we were waiting for the school bus to arrive Suddenly we get a call from the school ofice that the then school was going to be closed and were supposed to stay at home and study.

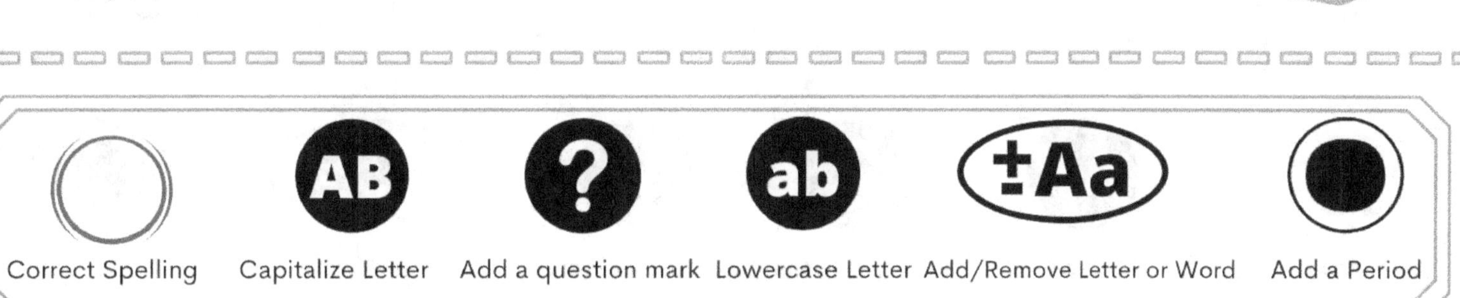

While i was walking down the road I saw a small puppy on the side of the Road, It was very small and cute. I picked up to the dog and took it home and we adopted it the same day and we kept its name as Bruno

Find the Errors & Fix the Grammar

Once there was a king who had built for himself a Castel where everything was made of gold The chairs, doors cutlery and even the Bed was made out of solid gold. when the sun used to shine on the castle it used to glow bright and yellow

I like playing soocer because scoring goals make me feel very nice and my team wins. we practice everyday so that when play against other Teams we can play at our very bets. The coach also helps me a lot to make my game better

Find the Errors & Fix the Grammar

 Correct Spelling  Capitalize Letter  Add a question mark  Lowercase Letter  Add/Remove Letter or Word  Add a Period

One day my friend came and asked me "Hey Jack, do you wantt to go watch a movie ? ". I wanted to go but had to fisrt ask my dad for permission. as soon as my dad came home I asked him if I could go watch the . He llowed so we both went and enjoyed a lot.

 Capitalize Letter  Add a question mark  Lowercase Letter  Add/Remove Letter or Word  Add a Period

Correct Spelling

my friend Jack went to see dolphins where they also jumping through hoops and balanced balls on their nose He show me a lot of photo's of him his family at the show where they got to see all this. Today I will also ask my Parents if we coulf go.

 Correct Spelling
 Capitalize Letter
 Add a question mark
 Lowercase Letter
 Add/Remove Letter or Word
 Add a Period

Our teacher us lots of candy today because it was childrrens day. I got 2 candy bars 3 caramel toffees. I hope everyday is children's day so that we get to eat these sweet delicious treats regularly.

 Capitalize Letter
 Add a question mark
 Lowercase Letter
 Add/Remove Letter or Word
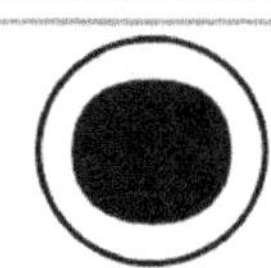 Add a Period

do you know that exercise helps us to regulate our body temperature Yes you may be surprised hear that when we sweat that means that ours bodies is trying to keep us cool.

Find the Errors & Fix the Grammar

One of the most important thing to do when you woke up is to make your own bed This ensures that we learn discipline and aslo keep our room tidy clean. So the next time when you wake up then to go make your own bed.

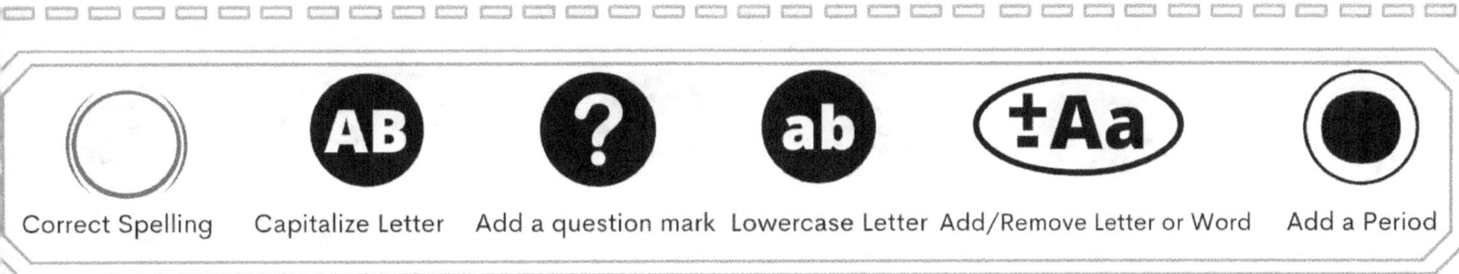

When I first saw Jellyfish at the beach I thought that it's made of jelly or candy because it looks very cool. but my teacher told me that the jellyfish is very poisonous and should never be touched as they can sting person.

Find the Errors & Fix the Grammar

My Friend got a new video game and she invited me to come over house to play. The game was really cool as had fast cars which you need to race againstt each to win and the person who wins gets the trophy

Today when I reached home I rang the belll and my dad opened the door with a Present in his hand. He told me to close my eyes, when opened my eyes I saw that he had got me brand new baseballl bat. I hugged him and thanked for the present.

When I walked into school Today we saw that there is a new swing in the Playground, Seeing swing our faces lit up with the joy and we wanted to go and play right there and then but first we needed to go bacc into class and finish studying.

The neighbors dog always comes over to my houze, I think he likes to hang around with me and my brothre. We feed him some peanut butter which he eatens in like under 2 seconds and wags his tail with joy.

| Correct Spelling | Capitalize Letter | Add a question mark | Lowercase Letter | Add/Remove Letter or Word | Add a Period |

Whenever we go to the restatrrant its very hard for my friends to order as they do not know what to eat They usually end up getting to the french fries with a burger and a lemon Soda and a apple pie for dessert.

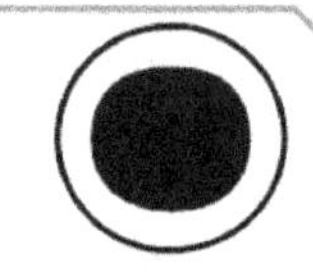

| Correct Spelling | Capitalize Letter | Add a question mark | Lowercase Letter | Add/Remove Letter or Word | Add a Period |

The desert is the very big place and is extremely hot. It's very hard for anything to grow there so mostly one will not find trees animals in large numbers. Also there is limited supply of Water which is the main reason for less vegetation.

reading newspaper everyday is a nice habit to form as we get to know what is going around in the cntry and also in our very own state This not only improves our ability read but also keeps us up to to the date.

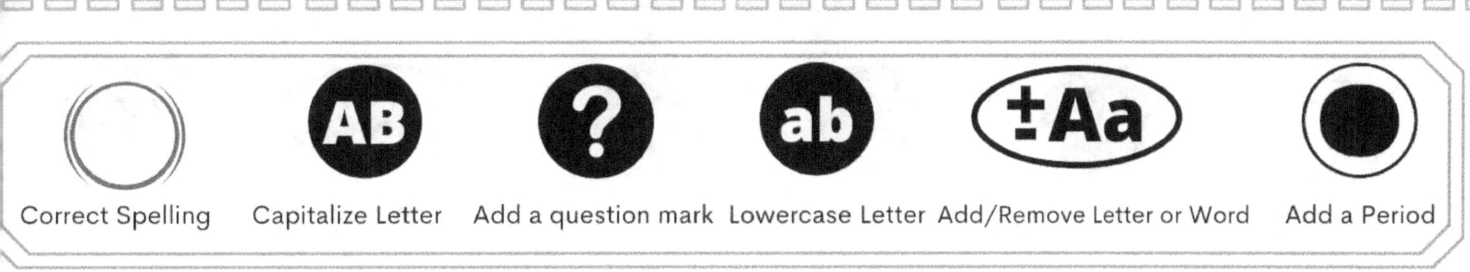

My dad has the best perfume ever, It Reminds me of the Ocean and also takes me to the beach virtually. He always uses it before he to the office to work. I have used it many times after he is left the home for Work.

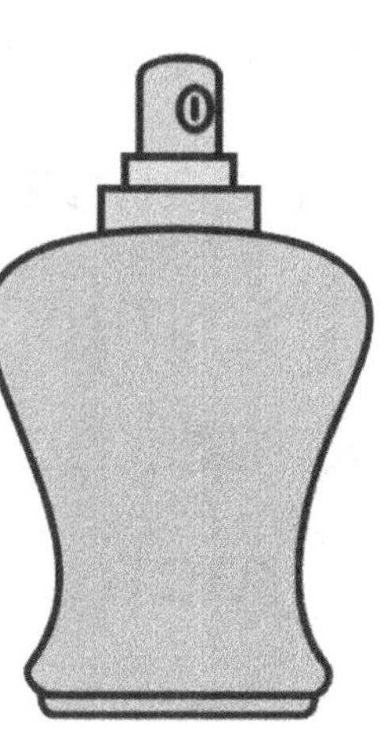

○ Correct Spelling **AB** Capitalize Letter **?** Add a question mark **ab** Lowercase Letter **±Aa** Add/Remove Letter or Word ● Add a Period

The wheels of a Truck are very Huge and strong. I asked my dad "How much is their height ", He told me that it has a height of about 32 inches weighs 130 pounds.

○ Correct Spelling **AB** Capitalize Letter **?** Add a question mark **ab** Lowercase Letter **±Aa** Add/Remove Letter or Word ● Add a Period

the carpet in my house has to be cleaned because my little Brother jack spilled all of his milk it. He was running around and knocked over a tumbler of nilk which fell directly onto it.

Find the Errors & Fix the Grammar

Our Grandpa has a big old car which is red.
He usually rides it with the radio full volume
and plays country music on it. the car can go
to very high speed and makes a lot of noise
on road.

My hobby is to collect caps, I have over 22
Caps in my cabinet. They range a variety of
colors such as bright yellow, Blus, grey and
many others. now I am planning to purchase
some more

 Correct Spelling  Capitalize Letter  Add a question mark  Lowercase Letter  Add/Remove Letter or Word 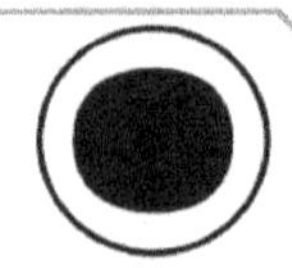 Add a Period

Food waste is a big Problem in our country, Everyday tons of food is wasted which been fed to the needy. so the next time you take food only take the quantiti which you need and try to minimize foud wastage.

 Correct Spelling  Capitalize Letter  Add a question mark  Lowercase Letter  Add/Remove Letter or Word 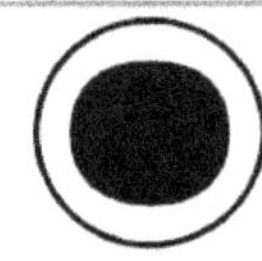 Add a Period

Do you know how long it takes for plastic to decompose , It takes about a 1000 yers for plastic to fully decompose Next time when you are at the shopping mall do not ask for a plastic bag to keep your belongings.

Find the Errors & Fix the Grammar

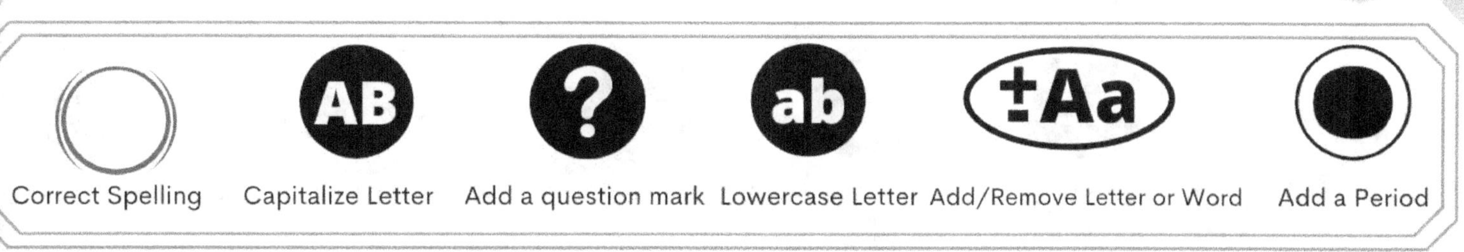

day before yesterday Michael took a watermelon from the farm to his home. On the way he dropped the Watermelon a couple of times and. it almost become like pulp when we cut it to eats.

There is a great offer going on at the locals store on video games They are offering up to 50 percents discount on popular games when you buy two and if you buy threi then they will is give you a keychain free.

Find the Errors & Fix the Grammar

Suzie wanted to go fishing so we went to the Nearbuy lake and tried fishing for the first time. We put fishing rod into the lake and waited patiently for to catch something Much to our surprise few minutes later we had a big fish in our hands.

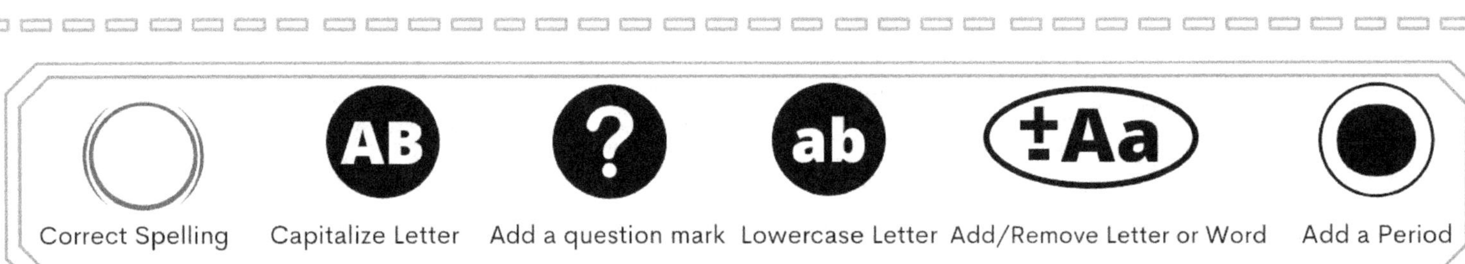

if you want to see stars in the night then I suggest to you that go to a mountain or the country side where there is less pollutions. We can sea more than a thousand twinkling stars night over there.

18

Correct Spelling   Capitalize Letter   Add a question mark   Lowercase Letter   Add/Remove Letter or Word   Add a Period

The Fisrts time i traveled by plane I was really excited to fly. I sat near is the window seat to watch everything. We got to see the clouds, the Ocean and a lot of things from high above the ground

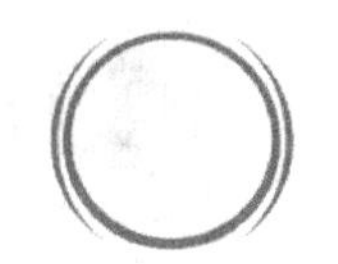     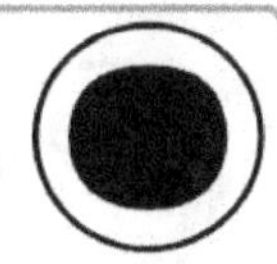

Correct Spelling   Capitalize Letter   Add a question mark   Lowercase Letter   Add/Remove Letter or Word   Add a Period

Matt was such a good baseball Player that one day he hits the ball so hard that we could not find it and was lost. Whenever he comes to play witth us we need to have at least a few balls because Matt hits so many home runs.

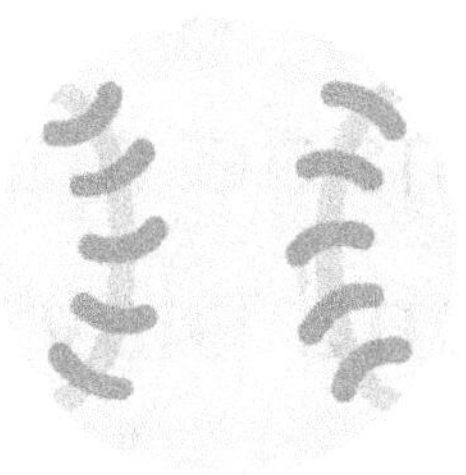

19

Find the Errors & Fix the Grammar

a lady once had more than 25 cats living with her in her home. Everyone used to go their to pet those cute little cats and also give them treats. she became really famous for having so many cats in her house

When I Was a kid we decided to move to a new city because my dad got a new job. The city was vely beautiful and had big building. I made many friends and invited home to study and play.

20

Find the Errors & Fix the Grammar

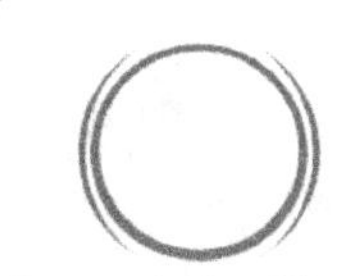

When the winter arrives the whole nieghbourhood has a snowman makings competition, Whoever makes the best looking wins the trophy and gets choose the next year's winner.

- -

Last summer my sister decide to Learn the piaono. She taking daily classes and perfected her skills. Today we went to her school to see the shows in which she was performing, It made parents really Proud.

Find the Errors & Fix the Grammar

If you want to make a good salad then you must know one thing, What do you think it is ?, its that a good salad always has good dressing which makes it even tasteirr. Next time you make some make sure to get a hold of a nice dressing like thousand island.

My friend brother was getting married this years, So we decided to plan a little ssurprise party. We called all of his best freinds and a lot of good food. We also put on good. music and danced the whole night.

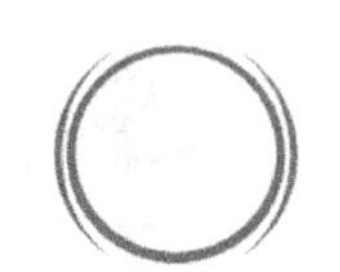     

Correct Spelling Capitalize Letter Add a question mark Lowercase Letter Add/Remove Letter or Word Add a Period

For the past few days it been raining quite a lot and has not stpped It is so hard to even go out and buy Groceries and daily essentials. Even the umbrella is of. no use at this time because the winds are so strong.

Correct Spelling Capitalize Letter Add a question mark Lowercase Letter Add/Remove Letter or Word Add a Period

When we got a little Older we were allowed to go inside the school lab. It was such a cool places because we got do a lot of exciting experiments with chemicals and had the oppurtunity to learn and fun.

Find the Errors & Fix the Grammar

my mom always tells me to eat broccoli but I just do not like it and I not think any kid Likes it either. Instead give me chocolate, burger and pizza as I will not create any trouble and eat them quietly.

During the summer vacations many people like to go to the parks and Also to the beaches to cools down. You should also remebr to keep drinking watrr and. hydrating your body as the temperature is high.

Find the Errors & Fix the Grammar

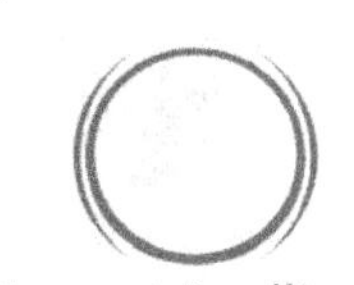 Correct Spelling  Capitalize Letter  Add a question mark  Lowercase Letter  Add/Remove Letter or Word 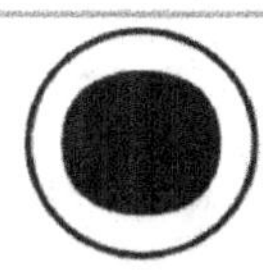 Add a Period

Not wearing socks and running is a Bad idea beacasue it caused me a lot of Rashes and some small cuts on my feet. It's always recommended to wear socks so that you can aviod this

 Correct Spelling  Capitalize Letter  Add a question mark  Lowercase Letter  Add/Remove Letter or Word Add a Period

Jack had a lot of ants in his backyard, we used to be afraid to go back there as those ants may bite us, it used to sting a lot when an ant you. They used be in hundred during the rainy seasom and would occasonaly come inside the house.

25

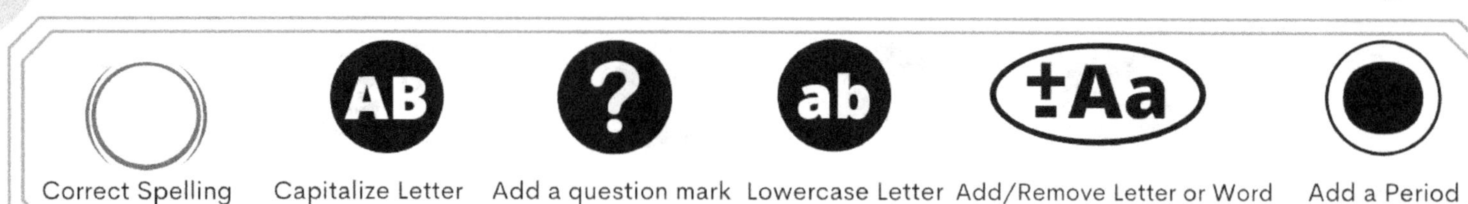

Do you Know what is the hardest material in the world, its the diamond which is clearly the most strongest object in the world, Also an interesting fact is that the diamond is to cut another diamond.

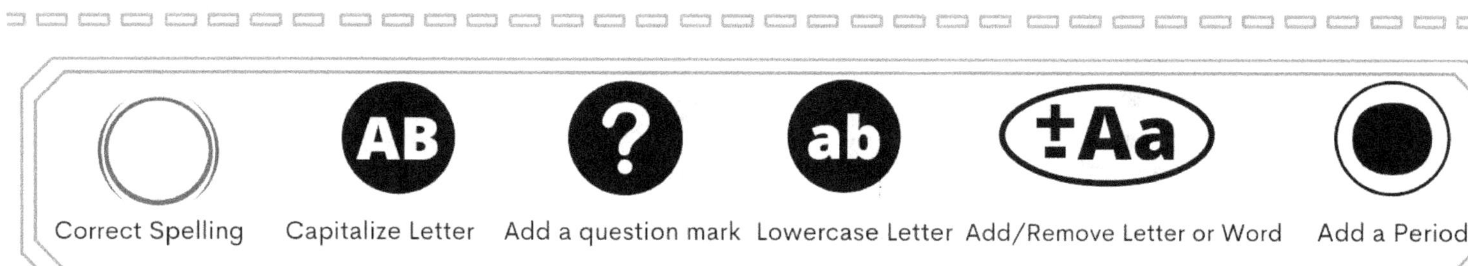

My favourite jacket is my black leather jackat which my father gave me when i turned 7. i wear it with him when I go for my bicycle ridess and also to the park where it gets little dirty but its okay because maom takes care of the stains.

Find the Errors & Fix the Grammar

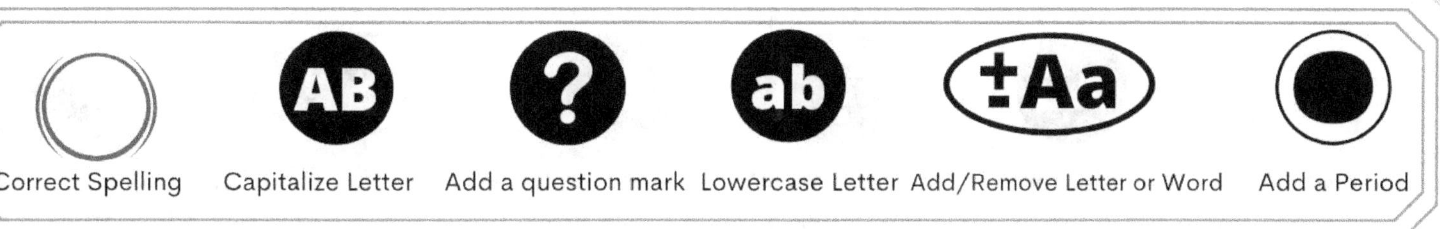

Me and my friemds love taking the bus to
school as we get to sing a lot songs and also
play Games when we are on our way. The
bus driver is a nice guy and he drives it very
safely, we also bring along snacks so we
can munch along the way.

Last month we went on a school trip to the
farm where we say so many smal animals
and some really big ones. like Horses, cows.
We got to plaay with little chickens, ducks
and also ate a nice lunch.

Find the Errors & Fix the Grammar

let me ask you something, How do you thimk the Dinasaurs went extinct . What happened was that a huge asteroid came crashing down to the Earth and wiped them straight off the face of the earth and made them extinct

It's aways so nice to see the rainbow after it has rained and then a brigt sun comes out, I always like to count the Colors of the rainbow beecause it is so vibrant and majestic and it totally makes my day and my dog also likes to watch them

28

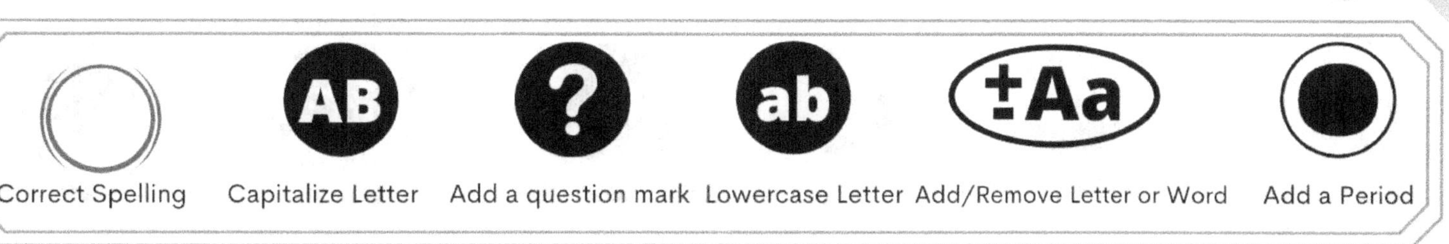

Skipping Stones is more than just skill but its an art, have you ever seen amyone skip a stone on the lake. it's so soothing see a stone skip soo many times. The conditions have to be realy proper such as the angle of the throw and the calmness of the water.

mount Everest is the earth's tallest mountain and it stands at a stagering 8,848 m. The first people to Clim it successfully are tenzing norgay and edmund hillary who climed it on 29th May 1953

Recently on my Birthday my dad gifted me brand new bicycle. I was so excited to show it to my friends so I went to their house on my Yellow cycle which was soo fast and also had cushioned seets. All of my friends congratuleted me and wanted to try it.

The Battery on my remote control car was low so we went to the sttore to buy a new one, But the store did not them so we had to travel for 1 hour to find a to new battery that could fits in my toy car.

Find the Errors & Fix the Grammar

 Correct Spelling    Capitalize Letter    Add a question mark    Lowercase Letter   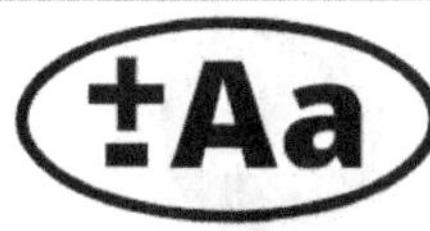 Add/Remove Letter or Word    Add a Period

Let me ask you someting do you knw how many minutes are there in a day, Take a guess. You willl be fascinated to know that there are 1,140 minutes in one day so better utilize them properly.

 Correct Spelling    Capitalize Letter    Add a question mark    Lowercase Letter    Add/Remove Letter or Word   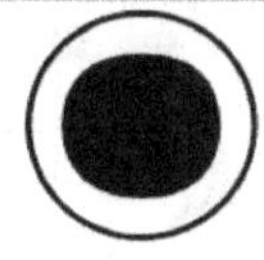 Add a Period

My dog loves to be in the pool and likes it when he in water. Every day in the summer he just sits there for hourrs and hours and we literally have to have pull him out and blow dry her because she has a lot of hair.

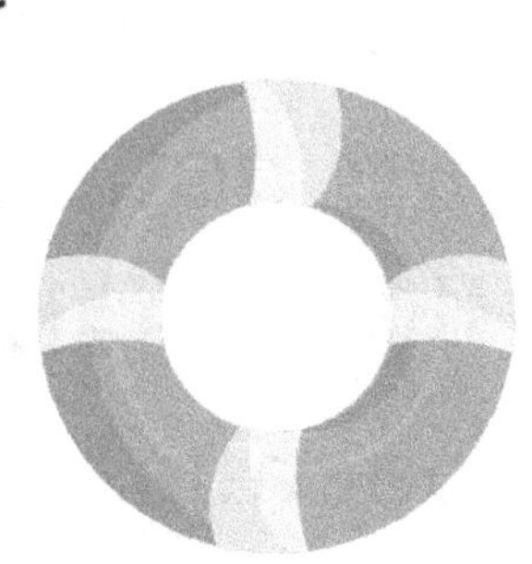

Find the Errors & Fix the Grammar

 Correct Spelling  Capitalize Letter  Add a question mark  Lowercase Letter  Add/Remove Letter or Word 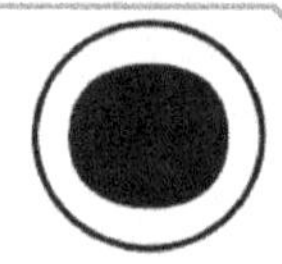 Add a Period

My math teacher is my favorite Because he teaches us short tricks to solve big problems, I like doing addition, subtraction, multiplicattion but when it comes division its really Hard and does take some practice to master.

 Capitalize Letter  Add a question mark  Lowercase Letter  Add/Remove Letter or Word 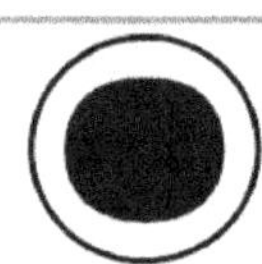 Add a Period

We heard a loud Bang outside and when we went outside to check what was happpened we noticed that there was a fighter jet that flying above us. The sound it makes is because the jet breaks speed barrier of sound and because its so fast

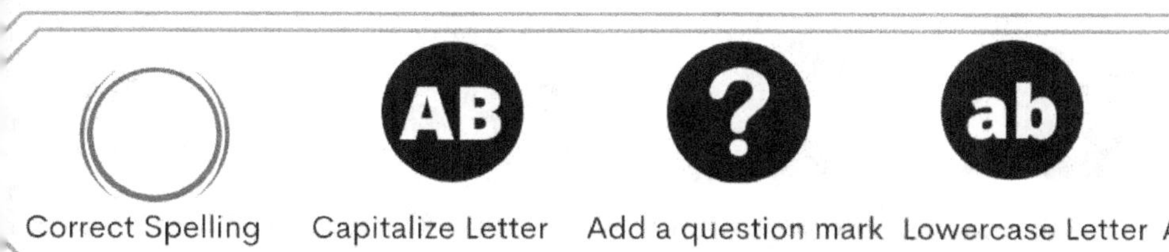

My brother likess to eat banana's so much that we got him a Birthday cake which was shaped like a banana. he liked our joke so much that he laughs for minutes, After which we all enjoyed this big bananna cake.

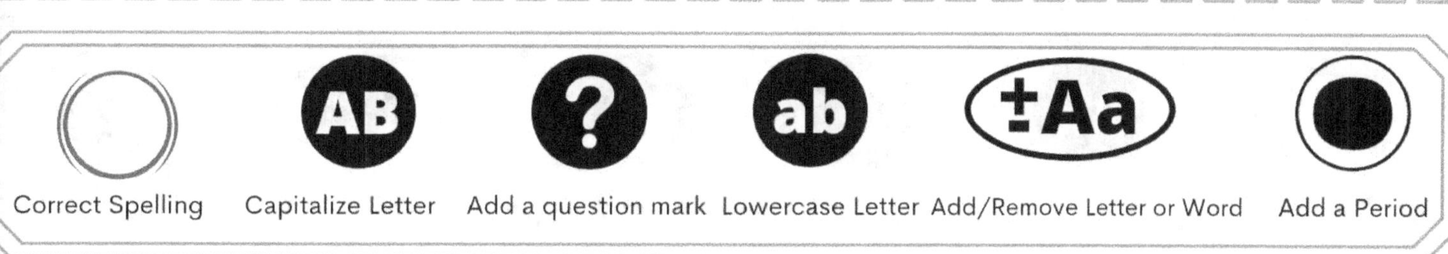

when we were kids my brother and I got in trouble for coloring the walls. of the house with crayon. We made dols, cats, dogs and different aninals on the walls of the house which made ours mom very Angry and she grounded us to for a week.

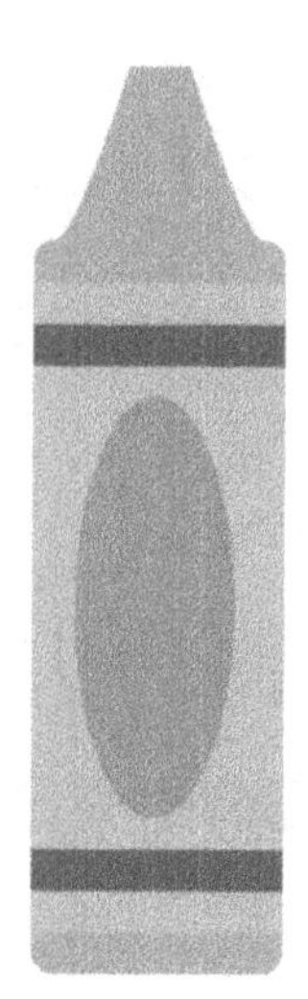

Find the Errors & Fix the Grammar

there was a frog outside toms house which used to make noise every night and did not let them sleep. they tried finding this green frog in the mornimg but he was so clever he went used hide in a hole while they werre searching for him.

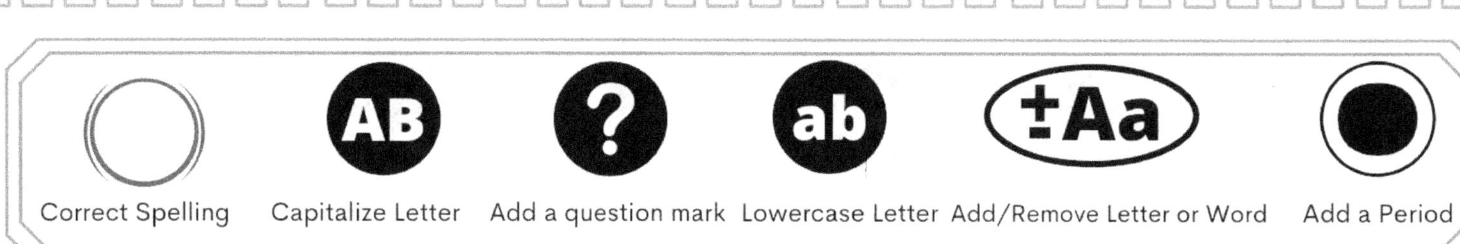

We finished ourr exams today and wanted to enjoy ourselves after such a stressfull week , so we all went to the carnival where us sat on many rides and saw a lot shows which were very fun

Find the Errors & Fix the Grammar

ny little sister likes to build these cute animals like dogs, swans turtles from clay. But the probllem is that she spoils al of her clothes when she plays with Clay and then mom has to have wash her clothes for hours o remove the Stains.

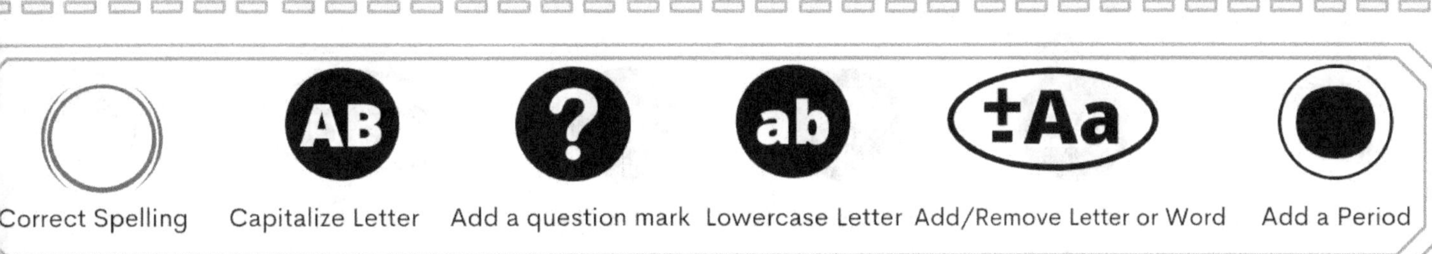

used to Watch the cartoon channel whole lay but one day my friend show me the ports chanel and I was so fascinated by asketbal that from that day we both went layed basketball and to this day we been egularly playing it.

Find the Errors & Fix the Grammar

There was man named Bob who used to go to the park and just close his Eyes and sing the whole day, after few days he stopped coming and everyone was surrprised that where did he go till this day nobody knows who he was and where did he go.

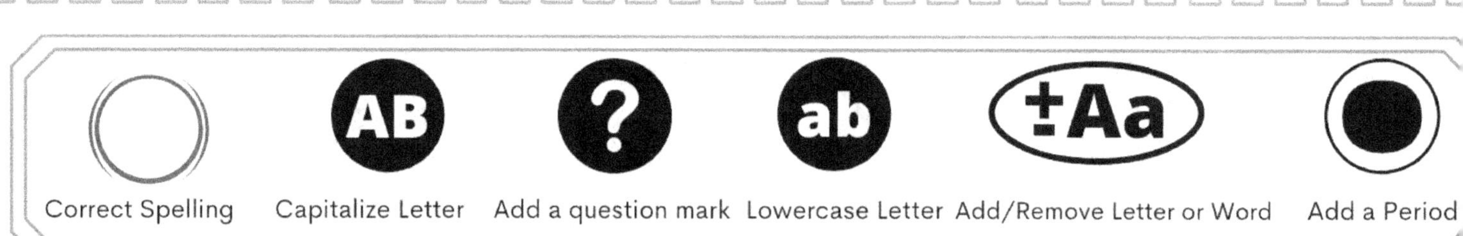

there are two ways to eat a cereal, Let me ask you which ones you prefer ?, do you like to put then milk over the cerreal or do you prefer to put the cereal over the Milk.

Find the Errors & Fix the Grammar

When it gets very cold and chilly during winter me and my broter bring some wood over and put it the fireplace after which we all sit down the in front of it and enjoy some delicious hot choccolate.

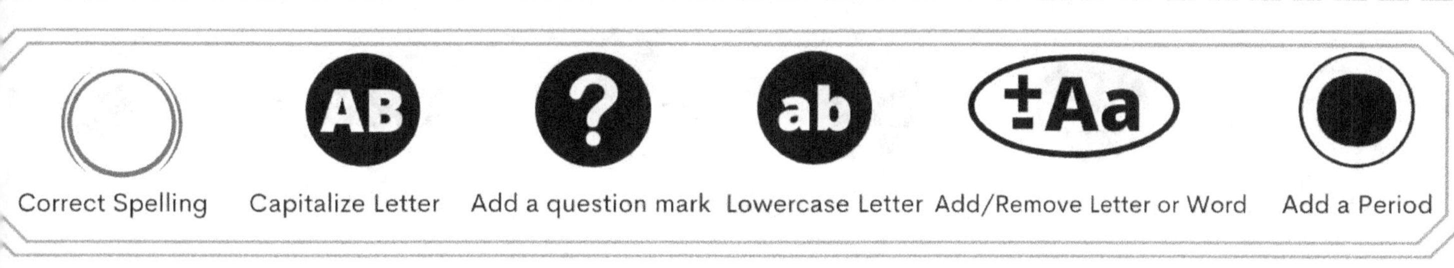

the first time mandy sat on a boat she was very scared that she will fall into the river. We all wore lifejacket's so even if we fell the lifejacket would save us and we us could swim easily

Find the Errors & Fix the Grammar

Santa claus had left us some candy near the christmas tree and also there was a small gidft which I opened and found that it had my favourite toy truck inside of. I playing with the truck for the rest the day and was very happy.

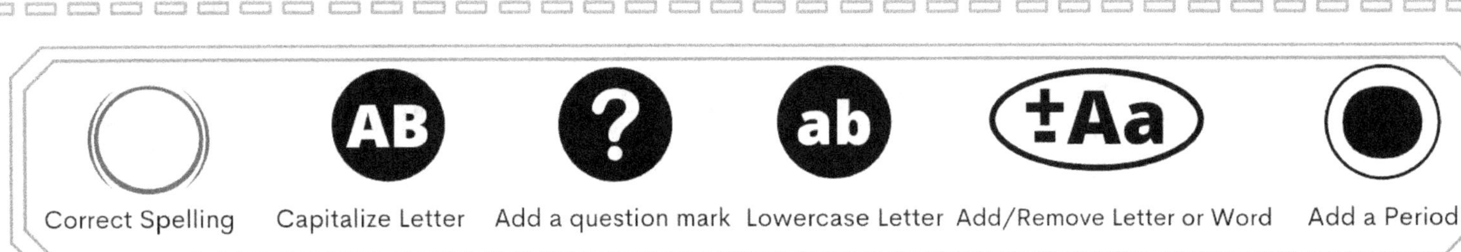

the last time we went to new york was to visit my grandmother who staying there. She made us some crunchy cokies and also made me a wool sweater which I can wear in winter

 Correct Spelling  Capitalize Letter  Add a question mark  Lowercase Letter  Add/Remove Letter or Word  Add a Period

Our school music teacher arranched for a musical which he would direct, There were 20 people who participated and in all of them had to a sing to get it. Finnally after the rials were done only best 10 got selectted nd I was one of them

 Capitalize Letter  Add a question mark  Lowercase Letter  Add/Remove Letter or Word  Add a Period

One of everyone's favourite hobby nowadays is play with slime and the kid love it. The real work is for the parents who have to then clean it up latter and its very difficult to do so

 Correct Spelling
 Capitalize Letter
 Add a question mark
 Lowercase Letter
 Add/Remove Letter or Word
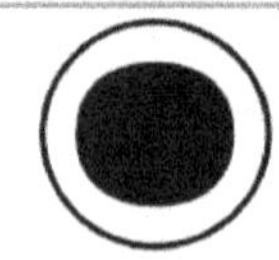 Add a Period

My cousis came over from another state and stays with us this spring break. They are both olders to me so they teach me a lot about sports, cars many other things, It makes I happy when they are around

 Correct Spelling
 Capitalize Letter
 Add a question mark
 Lowercase Letter
 Add/Remove Letter or Word
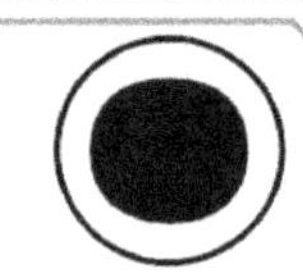 Add a Period

we took a taxi from the Library to the downtown area and when the taxi ride was very fun because we got to sea different monuments important buildings which we could not if we took the subway.

Find the Errors & Fix the Grammar

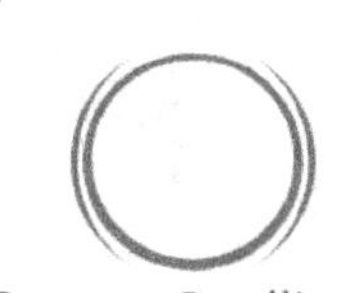 Correct Spelling  Capitalize Letter  Add a question mark  Lowercase Letter  Add/Remove Letter or Word  Add a Period

My dad llikes to play golf and he usually takes me with him whenever goes to the golf course, I tries swinging a couple of times but I am still Learning and will get better wit time.

 Correct Spelling  Capitalize Letter  Add a question mark  Lowercase Letter  Add/Remove Letter or Word  Add a Period

A boy named tristan was very scared to cross the road because he lacked courage. One fine day he told hinself that he will cross road and that day. he mustered up the power within to and the little boy crossed the road on his owm.

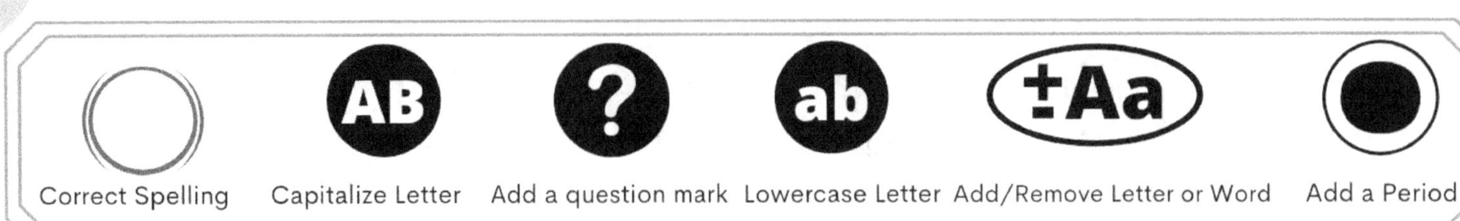

my friend Rob gave me 2 lollipops because it was his Birthday and he brought candy to the schol to give to the to children, But since i am his best friend he gave me 2 lollipops

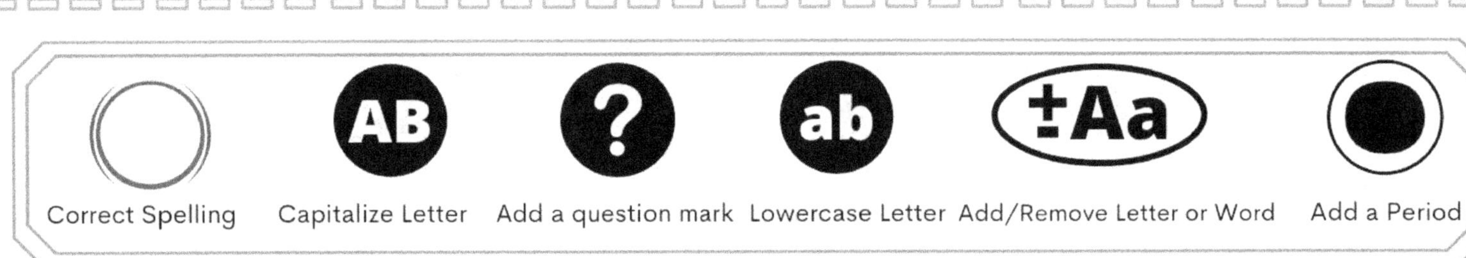

Once I went hiking with my sistter and brothers and we klimbed this huge mountain and so we could sees the clouds and also the stars. it was a really enjoyebla moment and made me like hiking even more.

Find the Errors & Fix the Grammar
Answers

Page 2 , First paragraph answers

1. In the first line the spelling should be 'with'.
2. In the second line the spelling should be 'sea'.
3. In the third line the spelling should be 'where'.
4. In the third line there should be an 'of' after 'lot'.
5. In the fourth line spelling of 'food' is wrong.
6. In the fifth line there should be a 'were' after 'we'.

Page 2 , Second paragraph answers

1. In the first line 'the' should have a capital 'T'.
2. In the first line 'thE' should have a lowercase 'e'.
3. In the third line the spelling should be 'prey'.
4. In the third line there should be period after 'force'.
5. In the fourth line there should be a question mark after 'weigh'.
6. In the fifth line the spelling should be 'replied'.

Find the Errors & Fix the Grammar
Answers

Page 3 , First paragraph answers

1. In the first line the spelling should be 'today'.
2. In the second line the spelling should be 'cheese'.
3. In the third line there should be an 'I' after 'while'.
4. In the fourth line one 'and' needs to be removed.

Page 3 , Second paragraph answers

1. In the second line the spelling should be 'noted'.
2. In the third line there should be an 'I' after 'which'.
3. In the third line the 'M' in 'Milk' should be in lowercase.
4. In the fifth line the 'to' should not be there.
5. In the sixth line there should be a period after 'home'.

Find the Errors & Fix the Grammar
Answers

Page 4 , First paragraph answers

1. In the first line the 'm' in 'me' should be capitalized.
2. In the first line the spelling should be 'sister'.
3. In the first line the 'F' in 'Fish' should be in lowercase.
4. In the fourth line the spelling must be 'goldfish'.
5. In the fifth line the spelling should be 'eat'.
6. In the sixth line there should be a comma after 'breakfast'.
7. In the sixth line there should be a period at the end.

Page 4 , Second paragraph answers

1. In the first line the spelling should be 'my'.
2. In the third line there should be 'to check' after 'mother'.
3. In the third line the word 'which' should not be there.
4. In the fourth line the 'F' in 'From' should be lowercase.
5. In the fourth line the spelling should be 'quickly'.
6. In the fifth line there should be a space between 'gave' and 'the'.

Find the Errors & Fix the Grammar
Answers

Page 5 , First paragraph answers

1. In the first line the 'R' in 'Raining' should be in lowercase.
2. In the second line there should be a period after arrive.
3. In the third line the spelling should be office.
4. In the fourth line 'then' should not be there.
5. In the fifth line there should be a 'we' after 'and'.

Page 5 , Second paragraph answers

1. In the first line the first 'I' should be capitalized.
2. In the second line the R in Road should be in lowercase.
3. In the third line 'to' should not be there.
4. In the fifth line there should be a period at the end.

Find the Errors & Fix the Grammar
Answers

Page 6 , First paragraph answers

1. In the second line the spelling should be 'castle'.
2. In the third line there should be a period after 'gold'.
3. In the third line there should be a comma after 'doors'.
4. In the fourth line the 'B' in 'Bed' should be lowercase.
5. In the fourth line the 'w' in 'when should be Capitalized.
6. In the sixth line there should be a period at the end.

Page 6 , Second paragraph answers

1. In the first line the spelling should be 'soccer'.
2. In the third line the 'w' in w'e' should be capitalized.
3. In the third line there should be a 'we' after 'when'.
4. In the fourth line the 'T' in Teams should be in lowercase.
5. In the fifth line the spelling should be 'best'.
6. In the sixth line there should be a period at the end.

Page 7 , First paragraph answers

1. In the second line the spelling should be 'want'.
2. In the third line the spelling should be 'first'.
3. In the fourth line the 'a' in 'as' should be capitalized.
4. In the fifth line there should be 'movie' after 'the'.

Page 7 , Second paragraph answers

1. In the first line the 'm' in 'my' should be capitalized.
2. In the second line there should be a 'were' after 'also'.
3. In the third line there should be a period after 'nose'.
4. In the third line the spelling should be 'showed'.
5. In the fourth line there should be an 'and' after 'him'.
6. In the sixth line the spelling should be 'could'.

Page 8 , First paragraph answers

1. In the first line there should be 'gave' after teacher.
2. In the second line the spelling should be 'children's '.
3. In the second line there should be 'and' after 'bars'.

Page 8 , Second paragraph answers

1. In the first line the 'd' in 'do' should be capitalized.
2. In the second line there should be a comma after 'temperature'.
3. In the third line there should be a 'to' after 'surprised'.
4. In the fourth line the spelling should be 'our'.
5. In the fourth line the spelling should be 'body'.

Page 9 , First paragraph answers

1. In the second line the spelling must be 'wake'.
2. In the second line there should be a period after 'bed'.
3. In the third line the spelling should be 'also'.
4. In the fourth line there should be an 'and' after 'tidy'.
5. In the fifth line the 'to' should not be there.

Page 9 , Second paragraph answers

1. In the first line the 'J' in 'Jellyfish' should be lowercase.
2. In the third line the 'b' in 'but' should be capitalized.
3. In the sixth line there should be an 'a' after 'sting'.

Find the Errors & Fix the Grammar
Answers

Page 10 , First paragraph answers

1. In the first line the 'F' in Friends should be lowercase.
2. In the second line there should be a 'to her' after 'over'.
3. In the third line there should be an 'it' after 'as'.
4. In the fourth line the spelling should be 'against'.
5. In the fourth line there should be 'other' after 'each'.
6. In the fifth line there should be a period at the end.

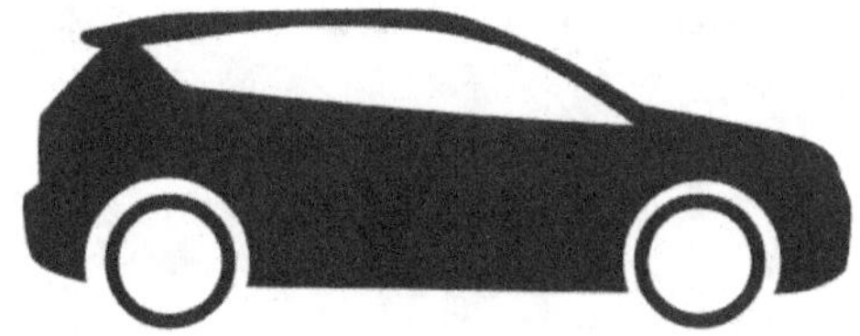

Page 10 , Second paragraph answers

1. In the first line the spelling should be 'bell'.
2. In the second line the 'P' in 'Present' should be lowercase.
3. In the fourth line there should be an 'I' after 'when'.
4. In the fifth line the spelling should be 'baseball'.
5. In the sixth line there should be 'him' after 'thanked'.

Page 11 , First paragraph answers

1. In the first line the 'T' in 'Today' should be in lowercase.
2. In the second line the 'P' in 'Playground' should be lowercase.
3. In the third line there should be a 'the' after 'seeing'.
4. In the third line there should not be a 'the'.
5. In the fifth line the spelling should be back.

Page 11 , Second paragraph answers

1. In the second line the spelling should be 'house''.
2. In the third line the spelling should be 'brother's '.
3. In the fourth line the spelling should be 'eats'.

Find the Errors & Fix the Grammar
Answers

Page 12 , First paragraph answers

1. In the first line the the spelling should be 'restaurant'.
2. In the third line there should be a period after 'eat'.
3. In the fourth line there should not be a 'to'.
4. In the fifth line there should be an 'an' before 'apple'.

Page 12 , Second paragraph answers

1. In the first line there should an 'a' instead of 'the' before 'very'.
2. In the third line there should be an 'and' after 'trees'.

Page 13 , First paragraph answers

1. In the first line the 'r' in 'reading' should be capitalized.
2. In the third line the spelling should be 'country'.
3. In the fourth line there should be a period after 'state'.
4. In the fourth line there should be a 'to' after 'ability'.
5. In the fifth line there should not be a second 'to'.

Page 13 , Second paragraph answers

1. In the second line the 'R' in 'Reminds' should be lowercase.
2. In the second line the 'O' in 'Ocean' needs to be lowercase.
3. In the fourth line there should be a 'goes' after 'he'.
4. In the fifth line 'is' should not be there.

Page 14 , First paragraph answers

1. In the first line the 'T' in 'Truck' should be in lowercase.
2. In the first line the 'H' in 'Huge' should be in lowercase.
3. In the third line there should be a question mark after 'height'.
4. In the fourth line there should be an 'and' after 'inches'.

Page 14 , Second paragraph answers

1. In the first line the 't' in 'the' should be capitalized.
2. In the second line the 'B' in 'Brother' needs to be capitalized.
3. In the third line there should be an 'on' after 'milk'.
4. In the fourth line the spelling should be 'milk'.

<u>Page 15 , First paragraph answers</u>

1. In the second line there should be an 'on' after 'radio'.
2. In the third line 't' in 'the' should be capitalized.
3. In the fourth line the spelling should be 'speeds'.
4. In the fifth line there should be a 'the' before 'road'.

<u>Page 15 , Second paragraph answers</u>

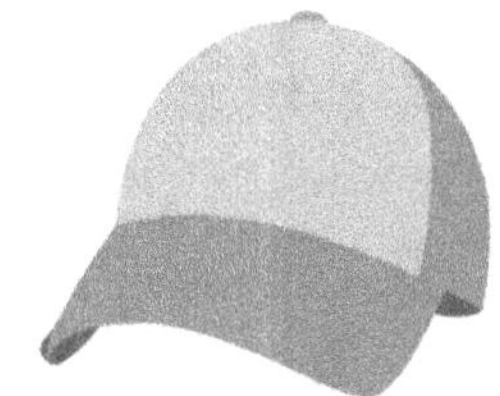

1. In the second line the 'C' in 'Caps' should be in lowercase.
2. In the second line there should be a 'from' after 'range'.
3. In the third line the spelling should be 'blue'.
4. In the fourth line the 'n' in 'now' should be capitalized.
5. In the fifth line there should be a period at the end.

Page 16 , First paragraph answers

1. In the first line the 'P' in 'Problem 'should be in lowercase.
2. In the second line there should be 'could have' after 'which'.
3. In the third line the 's 'in 'so' should be capitalized.
4. In the fourth line the spelling should be 'quantity'.
5. In the fifth line the spelling should be 'food'.

Page 16 , Second paragraph answers

1. In the second line there should be a question mark after 'decompose'.
2. In the second line the spelling should be 'years'.
3. In the third line there should be a period after 'decompose'.

Page 17 , First paragraph answers

1. In the first line the 'd' in day' should be capitalized.
2. In the third line the 'W' in 'Watermelon' should be in lowercase.
3. In the fourth line there should not be a period after 'and'.
4. In the fifth line the spelling should be 'eat'.

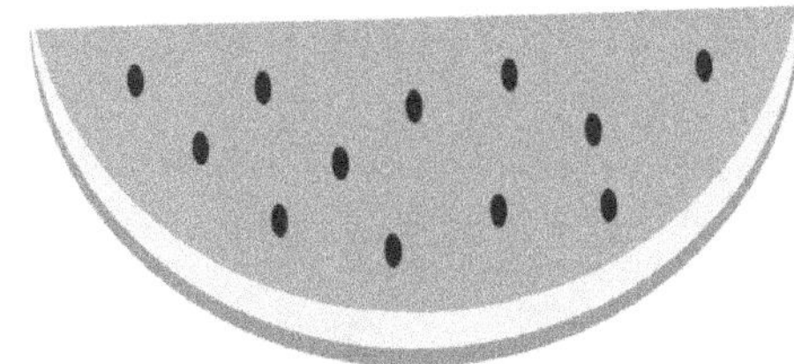

Page 17 , Second paragraph answers

1. In the first line the spelling should be 'local'.
2. In the second line there should be a period after 'games'.
3. In the third line the spelling should be 'percent'.
4. In the fourth line the spelling should be 'three'.
5. In the fifth line there should not be an 'is'.

Page 18 , First paragraph answers

1. In the second line the spelling should be 'nearby'.
2. In the third line there should be a 'the' after 'put'.
3. In the fourth line 'for' should not be there.
4. In the fourth line there should be a period after 'something'.

Page 18 , Second paragraph answers

1. In the first line the 'i' in 'if' should be capitalized.
2. In the third line the spelling should be 'pollution'.
3. In the fourth line the spelling should be 'see'.
4. In the fifth line there should be an 'at' after 'stars'.

Page 19 , First paragraph answers

1. In the first line the spelling should be 'first'.
2. In the second line there should not be an 'is'.
3. In the fourth line the 'O' in 'Ocean' should be in lowercase.
4. In the fifth line there should be a period at the end.

Page 19 , Second paragraph answers

1. In the first line the 'P' in 'Player' should be lowercase.
2. In the second line the spelling should be 'hit'.
3. In the third line there should an 'it' before 'was'.
4. In the fourth line the spelling should be 'with'.
5. In the sixth line the spelling should be 'home'.

Find the Errors & Fix the Grammar
Answers

Page 20 , First paragraph answers

1. In the first line the 'a' should be capitalized.
2. In the third line the spelling should be 'there'.
3. In the fourth line the 's' in 'she' should be capitalized.
4. In the fifth line there should be a period at the end.

Page 20 , Second paragraph answers

1. In the first line the 'W' in 'Was' should be in lowercase.
2. In the third line the spelling should be 'very'.
3. In the third line the spelling should be 'buildings'.
4. In the fourth line there should be a 'them' before 'home'.
5. In the fifth line there should be a period at the end.

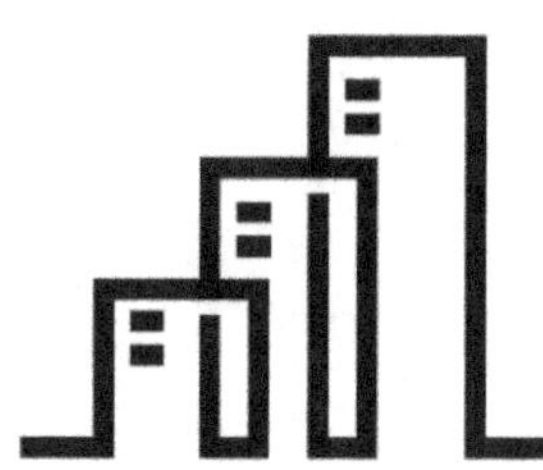

Page 21 , First paragraph answers

1. In the second line the spelling should be 'neighborhood'.
2. In the second line the spelling should be 'making'.
3. In the third line there should be 'snowman' after 'looking'.
4. In the fourth line there should be a 'to' after 'gets'.

Page 21 , Second paragraph answers

1. In the first line the 'L' in 'Learn' should be in lowercase.
2. In the second line the spelling should be 'piano'.
3. In the second line the spelling should be 'took'.
4. In the fourth line the spelling should be 'show'.
5. In the fifth line there should be 'our' before 'parents'.

Page 22 , First paragraph answers

1. In the third line 'i' in 'its' should be capitalized.
2. In the third line there should be an 'a' before the second 'good'.
3. In the fourth line the spelling should be 'tastier'.
4. In the fifth line there should be 'salad' after 'some'.

Page 22 , Second paragraph answers

1. In the second line the spelling should be 'year'.
2. In the third line the spelling should be 'surprise'.
3. In the fourth line the spelling should be 'friends'.
4. In the fourth line there should be 'had' after 'and'.
5. In the fifth line there should be no period after 'good'.

Find the Errors & Fix the Grammar
Answers

Page 23 , First paragraph answers

1. In the first line there should be 'has' after 'it'.
2. In the second line the spelling should be 'stopped'.
3. In the second line there should be a period after 'stopped'.
4. In the third line the 'G' in 'Groceries' should be lowercase.
5. In the fourth line there should be no period after 'of'.

Page 23 , Second paragraph answers

1. In the first line the 'O' in 'Older' should be in lowercase.
2. In the third line the spelling should be 'place'.
3. In the third line there should be a 'to' after 'got'.
4. In the fifth line there should be a 'have' after 'and'.

Page 24 , First paragraph answers

1. In the first line the 'm' in 'mom' should be capitalized.
2. In the third line the 'L' in 'Likes' should be in lowercase.
3. In the fifth line there should be a period at the end.

Page 24 , Second paragraph answers

1. In the second line the 'A' in 'Also' should be lowercase.
2. In the third line the spelling should be 'cool'.
3. In the fourth line the spelling should be 'remember'.
4. In the fourth line the spelling should be 'water'.
5. In the fourth line there should not be a period after 'and'.

Find the Errors & Fix the Grammar
Answers

Page 25 , First paragraph answers

1. In the first line the 'B' in 'Bad' should be in lowercase.
2. In the second line the spelling should be 'because'.
3. In the second line the 'R' in 'Rashes' should be in lowercase.
4. In the fifth line the spelling should be 'avoid'.
5. In the fifth line there should be a period at the end.

Page 25 , Second paragraph answers

1. In the third line the 'i' in 'it' should be capitalized.
2. In the fourth line there should be 'bites' after 'ant'.
3. In the fourth line the spelling should be 'hundred's '.
4. In the fifth line the spelling should be 'season'.
5. In the fifth line the spelling should be occasionally.

Find the Errors & Fix the Grammar
Answers

Page 26 , First paragraph answers

1. In the first line the 'K' in 'Know' should be in lowercase.
2. In the second line there should be a question mark after 'world'.
3. In the second line the 'i' in 'it's' should be capitalized.
4. In the fifth line there should be 'used' after 'is'.

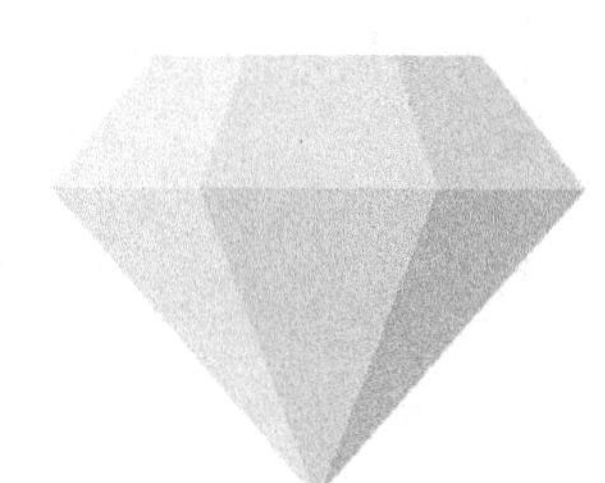

Page 26 , Second paragraph answers

1. In the first line the spelling should be 'favorite'.
2. In the second line the spelling should be 'jacket'.
3. In the third line the first 'i' s'hould be capitalized.
4. In the fourth line the spelling should be 'rides'.
5. In the fifth line there should be an 'a' after gets.
6. In the fifth line the spelling should be 'mom'.

Page 27 , First paragraph answers

1. In the first line the spelling should be 'friends'.
2. In the second line there should be an 'of' after 'lot'.
3. In the third line the 'G' in 'Games' should be in lowercase.
4. In the fifth line the 'S' in 'Safely' should be in lowercase.
5. In the fifth line the 'w' in 'we' should be capitalized.

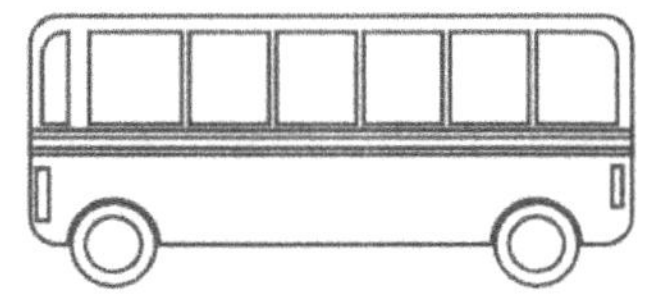

Page 27 , Second paragraph answers

1. In the first line the 'l' in 'line' should be capitalized.
2. In the second line the spelling should be 'small'.
3. In the third line there should not be a period after 'ones'.
4. In the third line the 'H' in 'Horses' should be in lowercase.
5. In the fourth line the spelling should be 'play'.
6. In the fifth line there should be a period at the end.

Find the Errors & Fix the Grammar
Answers

Page 28 , First paragraph answers

1. In the first line the 'I' in 'let' should be capitalized.
2. In the first line the spelling should be 'think'.
3. In the second line the 'D' in 'Dinosaurs' should be in lowercase and spelling should be 'Dinosaurs'.
4. In the second line there should be a question mark after 'extinct'.
5. In the fourth line the 'E' in 'Earth' should be in lowercase.
6. In the sixth line there should be a period at the end.

Page 28 , Second paragraph answers

1. In the first line the spelling should be 'always'.
2. In the second line the spelling should be 'bright'.
3. In the third line the 'C' in 'Colors' should be in lowercase.
4. In the fourth line the spelling should be 'because'.
5. In the fifth line there should be a period at the end.

Page 29 , First paragraph answers

1. In the first line the 'S' in 'Stones' should be in lowercase.
2. In the second line the spelling should be 'anyone'.
3. In the third line the 'i' in 'it's' should be capitalized.
4. In the third line there should be a 'to' after 'soothing'.
5. In the fourth line the spelling must be 'so'.
6. In the fifth line the spelling should be 'really'.

Page 29 , Second paragraph answers

1. In the first line the 'm' in 'mount' should be capitalized.
2. In the second line the spelling should be 'staggering'.
3. In the third line the spelling should be 'climb'.
4. In the third and fourth line the 't' in 'tenzing' and 'n' in 'norgay' should be capitalized.
5. In the fourth line the 'e' in 'edmund' and 'h' in 'hillary'' should be capitalized.
6. In the fifth line there should be a period at the end.

Find the Errors & Fix the Grammar
Answers

Page 30 , First paragraph answers

1. In the first line the 'B' in 'Birthday' should be lowercase.
2. In the fourth line the 'Y' in 'Yellow' should be lowercase.
3. In the fifth line the spelling should be 'seats'.
4. In the fourth line the spelling must be 'so'.
5. In the fifth line the spelling should be 'congratulated'.

Page 30 , Second paragraph answers

1. In the first line the 'B' in 'Battery' should be in lowercase.
2. In the second line the spelling should be 'store'.
3. In the third line there should be a 'have' after 'not'.
4. In the fourth line there should not be a third 'to'.
5. In the fifth line the spelling should be 'fit'.

Page 31 , First paragraph answers

1. In the first line the spelling should be 'something' and 'know'.
2. In the third line there should be a question mark after 'guess'.
3. In the fifth line the there should be a period at the end.

Page 31 , Second paragraph answers

1. In the first line the 'm' in 'my' should be in capitalized.
2. In the second line there should be an 'is' after 'he'.
3. In the third line the spelling should be 'hours'.
4. In the fourth line there should be a 'to' after 'have'.

Find the Errors & Fix the Grammar
Answers

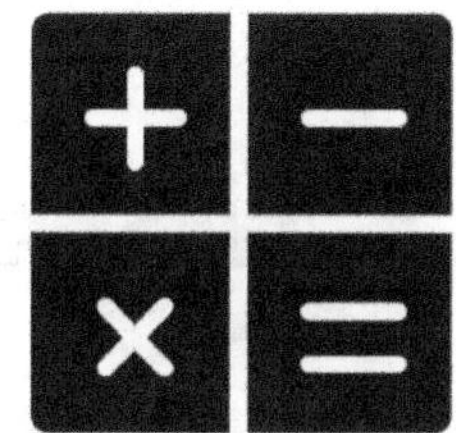

Page 32 , First paragraph answers

1. In the first line the 'B' in 'Because' should be in lowercase.
2. In the third line the spelling should be 'multiplication'.
3. In the fourth line there should be a 'to' after 'comes'.
4. In the fourth line the 'H' in 'Hard' should be in lowercase.
5. In the fifth line there should be a period at the end.

Page 32 , Second paragraph answers

1. In the first line the 'B' in 'Bang' should be in lowercase.
2. In the second line the spelling should be 'happening'.
3. In the third line there should be a 'was' after 'that'.
4. In the fifth line there should be a 'the' after 'breaks'.
5. In the sixth line there should not be an 'and'.
6. In the sixth line there should be a period at the end.

Page 33 , First paragraph answers

1. In the first line the spelling should be 'likes'.
2. In the second line the 'B' in 'Birthday should be in lowercase.
3. In the third line the 'h' in 'he' should be capitalized.
4. In the fourth line the spelling should be 'laughed'.
5. In the fifth line the spelling should be 'banana'.

Page 33 , Second paragraph answers

1. In the first line the 'w' in 'when' should be in capitalized.
2. In the second line there should not be a period after 'walls'.
3. In the third line the spelling should be 'dolls'.
4. In the fourth line the spelling should be'animals'.
5. In the fifth line the spelling should be 'our'
6. In the fifth line the 'A' in 'Angry' should be in lowercase.
7. In the sixth line there should not be a 'to'.

age 34 , First paragraph answers

1. In the first line the 't' in 'there' should be capitalized.
2. In the first line the 't' in 'toms' should be capitalized.
3. In the third line the 't' in 'they' should be capitalized.
4. In the fourth line the spelling should be 'morning'.
5. In the fifth line there should not be 'went' and a 'to' should be in front of 'used'.
6. In the fifth line the spelling should be 'were'.

age 34 , Second paragraph answers

1. In the first line the spelling should be 'our'.
2. In the second line the spelling should be 'stressful'.
3. In the third line the 's' in 'so' should be capitalized.
4. In the third line there should be 'we' in place of 'us'.
5. In the fourth line there should be 'of' after 'lot'.
6. In the fifth line there should be a period at the end.

Page 35 , First paragraph answers

1. In the first line the 'm' in 'my' should be capitalized.
2. In the second line there should be an 'and' after 'swan'.
3. In the third line the spelling should be 'problem'.
4. In the third line the spelling should be 'all'.
5. In the fourth line the 'C' in 'Clay' should be in lowercase.
6. In the fifth line there should not be a 'have'.

Page 35 , Second paragraph answers

1. In the first line the 'W' in 'Watch' should be in lowercase.
2. In the second line the spelling should be 'showed'.
3. In the third line the spelling should be 'channel'.
4. In the fourth line the spelling should be 'basketball'.
5. In the fourth line there should be an 'and' after 'went'.
6. In the fifth line there should be 'have' after 'we'.
7. In the sixth line there should be a period at the end.

Find the Errors & Fix the Grammar
Answers

Page 36 , First paragraph answers

1. In the second line the 'E' in 'Eyes' need to be lowercase.
2. In the third line the 'a' in 'after' needs to be capitalized.
3. In the fourth line the spelling should be 'surprised'.
4. In the fifth line there should be a period after 'go'.
5. In the sixth line the 'W' in 'Where' should be in lowercase.

Page 36 , Second paragraph answers

1. In the first line the 't' in 'there' should be capitalized.
2. In the second line the spelling should be 'one'.
3. In the second line the 'd' in 'do' should be capitalized.
4. In the third line the spelling should be 'the'.
5. In the third line the spelling should be 'cereal'.
6. In the fourth line the 'M' in 'Milk' should be in lowercase.

Page 37 , First paragraph answers

1. In the first line the spelling should be 'chilly'.
2. In the second line the spelling should be 'brother'.
3. In the third line there should be an 'on after 'it'.
4. In the fourth line there should be no 'the' before 'in front'.
5. In the fifth line the spelling should be 'chocolate'.

Page 37 , Second paragraph answers

1. In the first line the 't' in 'the' should be capitalized.
2. In the first line the 'm' in 'mandy' should be capitalized.
3. In the fourth line there should not be a second 'us'.
4. In the fifth line there should be a period at the end.

Find the Errors & Fix the Grammar
<u>Answers</u>

<u>Page 38</u> , <u>First paragraph answers</u>

1. In the first line the 'c' in 'claus' should be capitalized.
2. In the second line the 'c' in 'christmas' should be capitalized.
3. In the third line the spelling should be 'gift'.
4. In the fourth line the spelling should be 'favorite'.
5. In the fourth line there should be an 'it' after 'of'.
6. In the fourth line the spelling should be 'played'.

<u>Page 38</u> , <u>Second paragraph answers</u>

1. In the first line the 't' in 'the' should be capitalized.
2. In the first line the 'n' in 'new' and the 'y' in 'york' should be capitalized.
3. In the second line there should be a 'was' after 'who'.
4. In the third line the spelling should be 'cookies'.
5. In the fourth line there should be a period at the end.

79

Find the Errors & Fix the Grammar
Answers

Page 39 , First paragraph answers

1. In the first line the 'o' in 'our' should be capitalized.
2. In the first line the spelling should be 'arranged'.
3. In the third line there should not be an 'in'.
4. In the fourth line there should not be an 'a'.
5. In the fourth line the spelling should be 'finally'.
6. In the fifth line there should be a 'the' after 'only'.
7. In the sixth line the spelling should be 'selected'.
8. In the sixth line there should be a period at the end.

Page 39 , Second paragraph answers

1. In the first line the spelling should be 'favorite'.
2. In the second line there should be a 'to' after 'is'.
3. In the second line the spelling should be 'kids'.
4. In the fourth line the spelling should be 'later'.
5. In the fourth line there should be a period at the end.

Find the Errors & Fix the Grammar
Answers

Page 40 , First paragraph answers

1. In the first line the spelling should be 'cousins'.
2. In the second line the spelling should be 'stayed'.
3. In the third line the spelling should be 'older'.
4. In the fourth line there should be an 'and' after 'cars'.
5. In the fifth line there should not be an 'I'.
6. In the fifth line there should be a period at the end.

Page 40 , Second paragraph answers

1. In the first line the 'w' in 'we' should be capitalized.
2. In the second line there should not be a 'when'.
3. In the third line the spelling should be 'see'.
4. In the fourth line there should be an 'and' after 'monuments'.
5. In the fifth line there should be a period at the end.

Page 41 , First paragraph answers

1. In the first line the spelling should be 'likes'.
2. In the second line there should be a 'he' after 'whenever'.
3. In the third line the spelling should be 'tried'.
4. In the fourth line the 'L' in 'Learning' should be in lowercase.
5. In the fifth line the spelling should be 'with'.

Page 41 , Second paragraph answers

1. In the first line the 't' in 'tristan' should be capitalized.
2. In the third line the spelling should be 'himself'.
3. In the fourth line there should be a 'the' after 'cross'.
4. In the fourth line there should not be a period after 'day'.
5. In the fifth line there should not be a 'to'.
6. In the sixth line the spelling should be 'own'.

Page 42 , First paragraph answers

1. In the first line the 'm' in 'my' should be capitalized.
2. In the second line the 'B' in 'Birthday' should be lowercase.
3. In the third line the spelling should be 'school'.
4. In the third line there should not be 'the' after 'to'.
5. In the fourth line the 'i' should be capitalized.
6. In the fifth line there should be a period at the end.

Page 42, Second paragraph answers

1. In the first line the spelling should be 'sister'.
2. In the second line the spelling should be 'climbed'.
3. In the third line there should not be the first 'and'.
4. In the third line the spelling should be 'see'.
5. In the fourth line the 'i' in 'it' needs to be capitalized.
6. In the fourth line the spelling should be 'enjoyable'.